Colin Millar MBE was born and lives in Northern Ireland. The author has been in education for thirty-two years. During this period, he has been a teacher, education authority adviser, vice principal, principal and associate assessor with the Education Inspectorate. He became a widower in 2017 and took early retirement in 2019. He is the father of two sons, Conor and Ryan. Colin has been involved with supporting beginning teachers during their training and their early career. He decided to write this book to encourage young teachers and assist them to understand the actual classroom practice which promotes effective learning.

This book is dedicated firstly to my two parents, Tom and Jean Millar, for all their love, support and encouragement they gave me in my dream to become a teacher.

Secondly, it is dedicated to Mrs Alice Lennon, my mentor and role model, in becoming an effective special-needs educator.

Colin Millar MBE

PRACTICE MAKES IMPROVEMENT

AUSTIN MACAULEY PUBLISHERS™

LONDON • CAMBRIDGE • NEW YORK • SHARJAH

A CIP catalogue record for this title is available from the British Library.

ISBN 9781398421851 (Paperback)
ISBN 9781398421868 (ePub e-book)

www.austinmacauley.com

First Published 2023
Austin Macauley Publishers Ltd®
1 Canada Square
Canary Wharf
London
E14 5AA

I would like to thank AM Publishing, in particular Victoria, with all their patience and assistance in helping me publish this book.

Table of Contents

Preface

This book has arisen from the fact that in June 2020 I was forced to take early retirement from teaching in education following 32 years. Whilst this decision was hard to accept, I felt it was important to comply with my doctor's advice. If you are to be an effective educator, then you need to be functioning at 100%, anything less is an insult to your pupils.

Once I realised this by agreeing to retire, I was still operating as a professional by putting the needs of my pupils first. This was my mantra throughout my 32 years of teaching.

Over the years I was sent on many different training courses of the latest education approaches and guiding theories which happened to be in favour at any one time.

In this book, I hope to share those approaches or theories which I feel have made the most contribution to making my teaching more effective and my pupils' learning more efficient.

At no time do I claim that the approaches within this book are my own. If I remember the theory or approach, I will reference them.

As a teacher, I have taught in both mainstream and special school sectors. I have taught in composite and straight year group classes. I have taught from P1–Yr15. As well as that I have been an Advisory officer for the local education authority and an associate inspector with the ETI.

My hope is that this book will provide some useful guidance for teachers still active in the classroom.

Tell me and I forget
Teach me and I remember
Involve me and I learn
Benjamin Franklin

Chapter 1
Wardrobes and Coat Hangers

I have always thought of a child's educational journey as the building of their learning wardrobe. As we know wardrobes come in a wide variety of styles just as children differ from each other. The more learning experiences that child receives the more complex their learning wardrobe. The idea of a wardrobe is for storing clothes that an individual gathers up and uses. The bigger the wardrobe the larger the storage space the more clothes can be stored and used when required. The following table explains how the different aspects of education contribute to a child's learning wardrobe.

Education Stage	Wardrobe Contribution	Outcome	Wardrobe Construction
Early Years	Provides the different key pieces of wood for constructing the overall wardrobe.	The more enriching the early years' experiences the more pieces of wood and quality of wood is gathered for constructing the overall wardrobe.	 This photo by Unknown Author is licensed under CC BY-SA-NC
Primary	Coat hangers for hanging later and applied learning on.	The broader and more balanced the learning at this stage allows for many coat hangers to be placed in the wardrobe. It is on these that the applied learning is hung.	

Secondary	Different types of clothing are used at different times in different situations to be placed in the wardrobe.	The more applied and additional learning takes place the more different types of clothing can be hung.
Tertiary University or Vocational	This is where specific drawers are placed into the wardrobe for extremely specific types of garments used for specific occasions.	The more specific the drawers the better equipped the child will be for specific situations.

As you can see in this learning wardrobe that:

1. each stage is dependent on the previous stage.
2. it is important at each stage that the child is enabled to reach their full potential.
3. gaps at any stage will have detrimental and limiting effects on the next and overall achievement.
4. each stage is of equal importance in the overall construction of a child's learning wardrobe.

Seven Key Questions that educators at all stages should ask themselves when delivering their lessons and teaching programmes.

1. Do I really understand the children or young people I am teaching?
2. Do I really understand how my pupils learn or assimilate knowledge?
3. What role does my language either help or hinder my pupils understanding?
4. Do I encourage effective listening skills in my pupils?
5. Do I interact in the most effective manner with my pupils to assist their full engagement in the learning tasks?
6. Do I establish a stimulating, engaging and supportive learning space?
7. **Do I promote positive behaviour in my classroom?**

By examining the above questions educators can ensure that their delivery of learning tasks will enable maximum learning for the pupils and allowing their stage in the completion of their pupils learning wardrobes to be most effective.

Like all good carpenters, educators need to have the right tools to build the best and most useful learning wardrobe for each of their pupils. The following are the necessary tools they will need to have and fully understand how to use to construct the learning wardrobes.

Educators Toolbox of effective understanding of these teaching tools areas:

1. Child Development/Theories of Learning – Discussed in Chapter 2.
2. Boys/Girls Learning styles (Type A or B brain) – Discussed in Chapter 5.
3. Language in the classroom (Teacher and pupil) – Discussed in Chapter 6.
4. Listening skills in pupils – Discussed in Chapter 7.
5. Teaching Interaction Styles – Discussed in Chapter 8.
6. Positive Behaviour promotion – Discussed in Chapter 13.

It was only when I sat down and really asked myself the seven questions and then found out more about the areas within the toolbox that I can honestly say I started to become a more effective teacher in the classroom. The next chapters will look at each toolbox area individually and their relevance to the classroom and effective construction of the pupils' learning wardrobes.

Chapter 2
Learning Theories/Child Development

There have been many theories regarding how children learn over the past century. For educators to provide the best education for their pupils it is important to study all these theories and to take the best from each as no one theory can explain the complex process which is learning.

The following table outlines the major learning theories and extrapolates the importance for educators and learning in the classroom.

Theorist	Ideas	Important Points	Classroom Importance
Sigmund Freud (1856-1939)	Believed that personality develops in stages. Early childhood experiences influence on adult life.	Early experiences affect adult life.	Importance of early years experiences/early years education.
Montessori (1870-1952)	Children learn best by using their senses.	Children need to stimulate their senses to ensure effective learning	Hands on learning Structured Play Music, Art, PE
Piaget (1895-1980)	Children go through four stages of thinking that	Children should be given learning tasks suitable to	Child Centred Learning Fit the learning to the child.

	shape how they interact with the world.	their stage of thinking.	
Vygotsky (1898-1934)	Social contact is essential for intellectual development.	Children should have many opportunities for social interaction.	Group activities Social development programmes.
Erikson (1902-1994)	Personality develops in a series of crisis addressed stages.	Use of rewards and punishment to try affect a child's response to that crisis.	Positive Reinforcement Promoting Positive Behaviour Programmes
Skinner (1904-1990)	If a child's action brings about positive outcomes the child will most likely to be repeated.	A child's behaviour can be influenced by rewards and negative consequences.	Class reward systems Positive Pupil feedback

Let's look at child development studies and the relevance these have for educators in the classroom.

It is important for a teacher to understand human growth and development to best meet the needs of students, both collectively and individually. By understanding typical patterns of growth and development, teachers are better equipped to make appropriate educational choices. By understanding child (and adolescent) development, a teacher can make the most appropriate decisions possible about expectations for students, how to best have students engage with the material, and how to push students to grow academically, emotionally, and socially.

The following are the most relevant facts from child development studies that I feel are most relevant to educators.

Main Areas of Child Development

- cognitive development,
- social and emotional development,
- speech and language development,
- fine motor skill development, and
- gross motor skill development.

The seven different areas of learning and development in the matter of learning

- Communication and language development.
- Physical development.
- Personal, social, and emotional development.

Child development studies provide important guidance for the curriculum that as educators, we are to provide in our schools.
They also guide teachers in the classroom of the learning that are vital for children to grow and develop both physically and mentally.

- Literacy development.
- Mathematics.
- Understanding the world.
- Expressive arts and design.

What are the four specific areas of learning and development?

The four specific areas are:

- Literacy
- Mathematics
- Understanding the world

- Expressive arts and design

What are the prime areas of development?
What are the prime areas?

- Communication and language
- Physical development
- Personal, social, and emotional development

The above summaries indicate the great lessons that both Child development and Learning theories offer robust and direct guidance for all educators in terms of school curriculum areas and the methods of teaching.

Chapter 3
Nature and Importance
of Learning

Learning can and should be viewed as a lifelong continuous process and can occur at any age. Learning capabilities that human beings can be grouped into the following five groups.

1. Verbal Information – this refers to the knowledge of facts about a certain field of study. An important feature of verbal information must be presented in a manner appropriate to the learner. (**Child Centred Learning**)

2. Intellectual Skills – these are classified as the procedural knowledge which allows learning to take place.

(Factual Learning)

3. Motor Skills – these are the skills which allow for the physical development and movement performance.

(Physical Education)

4. Attitudes – these are the evaluative judgements by individuals about particular people or events.

Attitudes are only visible when associated with overt behaviours. Attitudes are learnt and not innate.

(Citizenship and Community Education)

5. Cognitive Strategies – play a part in the development of strategic knowledge allowing the finding of solutions to different problems or unstructured situations.

(Problem Solving, Personal Skills and Thinking Capabilities)

In the 1950s, Benjamin Bloom lead a team of psychologists which studied the range of learning behaviours.

In education circles, these studies are known as Bloom's Taxonomy. They arranged the learning behaviours into a hierarchy of overlapping learning domains. These domains are.

Cognitive (knowledge) – includes comprehension, organisational skills, factual knowledge.

Affective (attitude) – interests, attention, and values

Psychomotor (physical skills) – basic motor skills, coordination, and physical movement.

David Kolb's Learning styles research in the 1980s suggested the fundamental concepts by which a learner approaches a learning task or problem. He theorised that our learning style is based on the product of these two choices decisions.

1. How to approach a task.
2. The learner's emotional response to the experience.

Kolb's four learning styles included:

Diverging – these are individuals who prefer to watch rather than do.

Assimilating – these are logical individuals who prefer to have precise verbal information when solving problems.

Converging – these prefer technical problems and apply their learning to find solutions.

Accommodating – these prefer hands-on approach to solving issues or problems.

Finally, Carl Rogers Facilitation Theory of Learning. He stated that teachers should become facilitative teachers and understand the role played by the learner in the learning process i.e., the learner has an active role to play in any learning activity or process.

To be a facilitative teacher they should:

Set a positive classroom atmosphere.

Clarify the purpose of the learning task and the role of the learner.

Assist in the organisational and readiness of appropriate resources to the learner required for the Task.

> Kolb's learning styles relate to the importance of multisensory learning activities and are in relation to VAK research in the last decade.

Hopefully, this chapter outlines current classroom teaching and learning approaches and firmly places these in educational research and childhood development studies.

Chapter 4
Summary of Guidance for Effective
Learning from Theory

The following are the key main points for effective teaching that arise from both Learning and Child Development theories.

Roger's ideas directly link to the current thinking of WALT and WILF in lesson planning.

Success criteria being discussed with pupils before they carry out the learning task.

Plenary session and self-assessment at the end of lessons.

Structured Developmental Learning Programmes

Quality Early Years education

Practical Hands On learning activities

Parental Role is crucial

Teaching and Learning activity matches the child. NOT The child matches the teaching and Learning activity.	Pupil has an ACTIVE role in their own learning

Multisensory learning activities VAK are important	Assessment is important to provide precise child centred learning programmes

Effective Teachers and Classrooms

The most important teaching resource is the TEACHER! If the teacher does not get it right no amount of fancy equipment, games and ICT will help pupils to learn effectively. Over my 32 years' experience, I would say the following characteristics make an **effective teacher.**

Possesses a clear understanding of their subject.

Helps pupils to answer their questions by promoting problem-solving skills and not just providing them with the answer.

Provide imaginative interesting lessons which are multisensory and engage their pupils.

Supports learning with appropriate resources which assist the learning and not just used because they are there.

Makes sure that all their pupils are involved and progressing, regardless of their talents, abilities and learning styles.

Balances the need for didactic teaching with the need to facilitate pupil interaction and independent learning for a well-rounded teaching approach.

Continually assessing their pupils' understanding and progress in a non-formative manner.

Provides pupils with clear and specific awareness of their progress and role in their learning.

Sets homework that is relevant and builds upon the work already covered in class.

An outstanding teacher creates a classroom environment that is:

Both stimulating and challenging.

Respectful of all.

Organised in a manner that allows interaction in learning tasks.

Celebratory of the pupils' work by displaying the pupils 'work.

What are the attributes of an effective teacher?

Empathy – understands their pupils' learning styles and methods of learning.

Ambition – If teaching is not truly your vocation, your success as a teacher may will be limited.

Patience – remaining calm helps to provide A POSITIVE CLASSROOM ENVIRONMENT.

Energy – to energise the learning activities. If the teacher shows enthusiasm for learning this will reflect onto their pupils.

Passion – your passion will communicate itself to the students and create an engaging environment.

What do these all mean for the teacher in the classroom?

Make sure your face and body are animated during the lessons.

The shortest distance between two people is a SMILE!

Speak clearly using precise and understandable language.

Moving around the classroom during the lesson, rather than standing or sitting in one place throughout.

Always continue to learn and grow as a teacher. Seek out courses and qualifications through CPD to improve your knowledge and experience of teaching and learning. Learning is a lifelong journey.

Health Warning!

Ensure that you are maintaining a good work-life balance. Working hard is important, but it is just as important to make some time for yourself and enjoy your life outside work. If you are constantly stressed and running yourself into the ground, inevitably your lessons – and ultimately your pupils – will suffer as a result.

Classroom Management Checklist

Do bee!	Suggested Activity	Classroom Example	Do not bee!
Consistent in class rules and routines	Visual or Written class timetable		Critical of your pupils!
Encouraging and praising your pupils	Pupil Passport DO NOT USE CLASS CHARTS		False with your praise!
Caring towards your pupils.	Pupil Memory book		Sarcastic!

A role model for your pupils in your words and actions.	Teacher Contract		Insulting towards your pupils.
Ensure you always have your pupils' attention.	Green Circle or Attention Bell		Using tense or angry body language.
Use multisensory teaching methods.	VAK Methods/ Classroom displays		Monotone and didactic in your teaching
Able to start each day in a positive manner.	Morning Welcome Routine		Make assumptions about your pupils.

		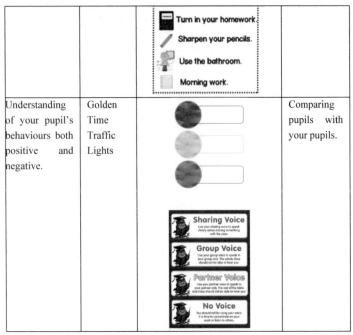	
Understanding of your pupil's behaviours both positive and negative.	Golden Time Traffic Lights		Comparing pupils with your pupils.

Explanation of the above activities.

Class Timetables

These are especially useful to provide pupils with an understanding of their day. They can be through visual pictures or for older children in written form. They help to develop organisational skills and independence in learning.

Pupil Passport

This allows teachers to reward individual pupils with reward stickers etc. By each pupil having their own passport, the information is private to the pupil themselves and maintains their dignity. DO NOT USE CLASS REWARD CHARTS as these are very unhelpful and can be damaging to pupils' mental well-being. Each pupil is unique in their learning journey and therefore should not be compared with others.

Pupil Memory Notebook

Teachers maintain a little notebook into which they record any event or happening reported by their pupils' lives. For example. Getting a new pet, going to visit granny, and going to the dentist. The teacher can then ask the pupil how they got on etc. This displays care and interest to the pupil. More importantly, it shows the pupil that they matter and are important. Easy way to promote self-esteem.

Teacher Contract

If the teacher expects their pupils to abide by an agreed contract, then they should also abide by one. This helps to underpin the value and relevancy of the class contract.

Green Circle and Attention Bell

These are simple ways that can be used and indicators that the teacher needs to have everyone's attention. When the bell is rung, or the green circle displayed then the pupils know to stop what they are doing and look at the teacher.

Classroom Displays

Classroom displays are useful as they:
Create colourful and stimulating learning environments.
Celebrate pupils' work and success.

Addressing Learning Styles

In general psychology, interest in learning styles goes back to at least the 1920s when **Carl Jung** proposed the theory of psychological types (**Sternberg and Grigorenko 1997**). In the field of education, the learning style concept has been recognised since at least the mid-1970s (**Griffiths 2012**).

Proponents of learning styles assessment in instruction believe that learning styles can be measured and used as a valuable teaching tool inside the classroom (for example **Sternberg, Grigorenko, and Zhang 2008**). According to these scholars, by diagnosing students' learning styles and matching them to teaching methods (for example for a 'visual learner', presenting information through pictorial illustrations), learning can be greatly enhanced.

In simple terms, there are three broadly identified learning styles:

- Visual (through the eyes)
- Auditory (through the ears)
- Tactile/Kinaesthetic (through touch/movement)

When a child is born typically the world is made sense of via tactile explorations. As the child grows, they begin to use both visual and auditory stimuli. On entering school, the child will have developed a prominent learning style. That is a preferred way of taking in information for processing in the brain.

Auditory Learners

(Revolutionarypaidela.com)

1. Auditory learners like to be read to.

2. Auditory learners sit where they can hear.
3. Auditory learners are most likely to read aloud or subvocalise when they read.
4. Auditory learners enjoy music.
5. Auditory learners acquire information primarily through sound.
6. Auditory learners are easily distracted by noises.
7. Auditory learners may not coordinate colours or clothes but can explain what they are wearing and why.
8. Auditory learners enjoy listening activities.
9. Auditory learners enjoy talking.
10. Auditory learners hum or talk to themselves or others when bored.

Classroom Implications

1. Will enjoy story time or listening to class novel.
2. Need to be seated close to the speaker or teacher.
3. They may need to talk to themselves when completing a task.
4. Will enjoy music lessons.
5. Will enjoy class discussions and debates in class.
6. Do not enjoy background noise as it distracts them.
7. They are able to listen and assimilate verbally presented information and instructions.
8. They will enjoy answering questions and not be shy to vocalise their opinions.

Tactile Learners

(Revolutionarypaidela.com)

1. Learns best when physically engaged in a 'hands-on' activity.
2. Bears down extremely hard with pencil or pen when writing.
3. Remembers best by writing things down several times.
4. Learns spelling by 'fingerspelling' the words.
5. Often is good at working and solving jigsaw puzzles and mazes.

6. Often does not like to read directions, would rather just do it.
7. Learns best when shown how to do something and then can do it.
8. Often prefers not to study at a desk.
9. Thinks better when given the freedom to move around.
10. Often needs frequent breaks during studying.

Summary

Whilst there are scientific discussions around these learning styles as an educator, I feel that they are important for the following reasons.

1. A class of pupils will not all learn the same way.
2. They underpin the need for a broad and balanced curriculum.
3. They also underpin the need for lessons to be delivered in a variety of ways to ensure the attention and engagement of the pupils in the task is maximised.

Classroom Implications

Include classroom activities that don't always require sitting at a desk.

Introduce simulations and roleplay where appropriate.

Allow pupils to practice technique rather than just verbally explaining it.

Provide frequent study breaks so they don't sit for long periods of time (mind gyms).

Use computers to combine learning with the sense of touch.

Use software they can interact with.

Utilise as much practical equipment as possible in the learning tasks.

Allow for stretching time (between lessons).

Chapter 5
Gender Issues in Learning

Studies show that boys learn differently than girls. Brain scans tell part of the story. In general, more areas of girls' brains, including the cerebral cortex (responsible for memory, attention, thought, and language) is dedicated to verbal functions. The hippocampus – a region of the brain critical to verbal memory storage – develops earlier for girls and is larger in women than in men. "That has a profound effect on vocabulary and writing," Gurian says.

In boys' brains, a greater part of the cerebral cortex is dedicated to spatial and mechanical functioning. So, boys tend to learn better with movement and pictures rather than just words, Gurian says. There are no differences between boys and girls in terms of what they can learn. "But there are," he says, "big differences in the way to teach them."

(*Michael Gurian, co-founder, Gurian Institute; author, The Minds of Boys: Saving Our Sons from Falling Behind in School and Life.*)

During my practice, I did notice the following general differences between most boys and most girls in their approaches to learning.

Boys	Girls	Classroom Implications to ensure effective learning
Boys prefer to learn by doing	Girls learn by watching and listening	Learning tasks need to include some practical elements and limited verbal. Lessons can involve high verbal content and limited practical.
Too much language can hinder a boy's learning.	Language is a girl's best friend	Verbal instructions should be short, precise, and delivered at different times during the task. Verbal instructions can be detailed and given at the start of the task.
Boys learn by trial and error	Girls are more methodical in their learning	Allow boys to experiment during learning activities so they come up with a plan for completing the task. Allow girls to plan first before completing the task.
Boys are motivated by external motivators	Girls are more intrinsically motivated	Boys will respond to praise and rewards during and after the task. i.e., Proximal Praise. Girls prefer to have more detailed praise after the completion of the task.
Boys tend to overestimate their abilities.	Girls tend to underestimate their abilities.	Ensure that boys clearly know the parameters of the learning task. Control risk-taking. Try to encourage girls to move outside of their comfort zones. Take risks.
Boys tend to rush at a learning task.	Girls are more cautious about learning tasks.	Break up learning tasks for boys into sections allowing them to complete the overall task more efficiently. Encourage girls to not overthink a task and to approach it more

		quickly than normal. (Reducing task completion time)
Boys can only do one thing at a time.	**Girls can multi-task**	Present boys with one activity at a time. Allow them to finish one task before introducing another. Girls can be given more than one task at a time.
Boys do not work well in all-male groups	**Girls work better at group work and collaborative tasks**	Boys do not work well in all-male groups when working on a shared task. Girls can work better in all-female groups. Mixed groups are the best combination for effective learning to occur.
Boys tend to have short attention spans	**Girls tend to be able to concentrate for longer periods.**	Remind boys during a task what they are meant to be doing and what the final goal is. Girls need only to be reminded near the end of the task.
Boys listening skills can be extremely poor.	**Girls listening skills are generally higher**	Fully ensure that boys have listened to the instructions and not just heard them. (Repeat, Rephrase, Recheck) Girls will not require as much checking
Boys tend to see the short-term goal	**Girls can see the long-term goal.**	Boys need to have tasks that have a definite end. Girls can link activities which join to give a final goal
Boys seek short term praise to keep themselves focused	**Girls prefer more focused praise**	As above boys need continual praise Girls need praise at the end of a task with more substance to the praise.

During my years in the classroom, I did however notice girls who displayed male characteristics and vice versa. So, taking the above theory and observations I came up with my own explanation for what I was seeing in my classroom.

There exist two brain types:

Type A – this was observed in most girls.

Type B – this is observed in most boys.

However, it was possible for there to be boys with Type A brains and girls with Type B brains.

Therefore, it was not necessarily a straightforward gender issue more of a particular brain type a person possessed.

Chapter 6
Teacher Communication

When communication is effective, both the student and the teacher benefit. Communication makes learning easier, helps students achieve goals, increases opportunities for expanded learning strengthens the connection between student and teacher, and creates an overall positive experience.

Teacher communication can either HELP or Hinder the pupils' understanding.

I have discovered the following hints that helped to make my communication skills effective in helping my pupils understand the verbally presented instructions and knowledge I was sharing with them.

Class Talk Tips

(**C**ommunication **L**etting **A**ll **S**tudents **S**hare **T**alking **and** **L**istening **K**nowledge)

1. Lower the background noise. All too often as teachers, we start to give instruction amidst a busy classroom. No wonder why a section of the pupils either do not complete the task or complete it in the wrong way.

WHEN GIVING INSTRUCTIONS OR A LEARNING FACT MAKE SURE THE CLASSROOM NOISE IS LOWERED.

2. Make sure that you have the attention of the class, group of children or individual child before speaking. This may seem so obvious and simple but many times during a busy class of 29, I would try to give instructions or engage children amid the clamour and chat. (Green circle in chapter 4.)

MAKE SURE YOU HAVE THE PUPILS' ATTENTION.

3. Repeat, Rephrase and Re-check. When presenting verbal information or instructions to ensure that the pupils have understood and are assimilating the information, carry out the 3Rs.

Example
Can you take out your maths books and turn to page 7.

Repeat – Can you take out your maths books and turn to page 7.

Rephrase – Take out your Maths Books. Turn to page 7.

Re-check – What are you taking out? What page will you turn to?

4. Emphasise keywords. In any verbally presented information, identify which words in the instruction which convey the meaning. When you have identified those when speaking slightly emphasise these words.

Example

Will the red group line up at the door?

*Identify keywords (shown in **bold**)*

*Will the **red** group **line up** at the **door**?*

5. Use Visual Cues – To assist your verbal instructions you can use visual cues to assist the understanding. These can be any of the following:
   - Pointing.
   - Relevant objects.
   - Pictures.
   - Photographs.

Example

Time to get your PE bags from your hangers at the back. Visual cues could be:

1. An empty PE bag.
2. point to the hangers at the back.

Health Warning!!!

DO NOT PRESENT THE VERBAL INSTRUCTION AND VISUAL CUES TOGETHER. THIS CAN CAUSE CONFUSION IN PUPILS' PROCESSING PROGRESS. EITHER SAY THE VERBAL THEN PRESENT THE VISUAL CUE OR VICE VERSA.

6. Pause between instructions and speak slower. – Especially in N Ireland we tend to speak very quickly, and we cram a lot of information into a short burst of verbalisation. Children's brains do not process at the same speed as an adult's brain. Therefore, if we speak too quickly some of the information will be missed resulting in the task not being completed correctly.

So, slowing down and leaving pauses gives the child's brain time to process and assimilate the information.

Example

Okay class, it is nearly home time. So pack all your stuff away and get your coats.

I once attended a CPD course where the speaker said that the brain likes information given in three chunks. This is the most effective way of the brain processing information. From that day, I always tried to divide my verbal instructions into three chunks.

1. Okay class, it is nearly home time.
2. So, pack your stuff away.
3. Now get your coats.

I would pause between each one and wait for each instruction to be followed before saying the next.

4. Ensure your vocabulary is known – I taught in P3 a school in East Belfast. I noticed that one of my pupils never engaged in the house corner. The corner was set up as a kitchen and the pupil just used to stand there. I was very worried and ask his granny who he lived with to come for a chat. After expressing my deepest concerns that there might be a learning difficulty (I was young and just out a few years!). I told her that he never engaged in the house corner kitchen. I remember she laughed and said she was so surprised as he was always under her feet or helping her in the scullery. BINGO, I realised that his granny called their kitchen the scullery. The next day, I told him I was going to play in the scullery corner. To my amazement, he started to fill the kettle and make a cup of pretend tea!!!

NEVER ASSUME, THE VOCABULARY YOU USE IS KNOWN BY YOUR PUPILS.

5. Be a wise **OWL**! As a teacher when you have given an instruction to pupils and you think they have not understood you often jump in with more words and verbalisation. These extra words will not help but hinder understanding.

So before jumping in be a wise OWL.

Observe

Wait

Listen

Usually around 10 seconds, which does not feel like a long time but believe me, it makes all the difference to the pupil.

By simply using the above approaches I was able to ensure that my language and verbal delivery of information was most efficient and enable my pupils to process and assimilate the information resulting in effective learning.

(Ref. Elkan Training Programme)

Chapter 7
The Bus Journey Analogy

Whilst I was working in the legacy South Eastern Education and Library Board, I was required to deliver INSET training to schools. When I was delivering the training course on communication, I devised the bus journey analogy to help explain the tips in the previous chapter can help or hinder learning.

Imagine that there is a bus inside each pupil's head. It is situated at the child's ear and it must journey to the bus station is situated at the brain's processing centre.

The words spoken by the teacher are the passengers boarding the bus. It is important that the passengers board in a logical manner and the bus knows its route to the brain station.

Issue	Effects on Process	Correction Tip(s)
Speaking too fast **CONFUSION**	Passengers instead of walking are running to get on the bus. Thus, they board and disembark in a confused order. **CONFUSION**	**Slow down.** (Allows an orderly boarding and therefore disembarkation. **Pause between instructions.** This allows the bus driver to board passengers in smaller groups. **UNDERSTANDING ACHIEVED**
Using no visual clues to assist instructions. **CONFUSION**	The driver has only verbal instructions which he needs to remember accurately. The driver will obviously forget the order and get lost. **CONFUSION**	**Use visual clues.** **This acts as a SATNAV and helps the driver check his verbal instructions and keeps the driver on the right road.** **UNDERSTANDING ACHIEVED**
Speaking in awfully long sentences. **CONFUSION**	**Emphasise keywords** There are so many passengers boarding at one time, and it is highly likely seats will be occupied in random order. This results in random disembarkation. **CONFUSION**	**Emphasise keywords** This allows the most information words to be given a Disney fast track ticket. This enables the most important words to board first and disembark first. **UNDERSTANDING ACHIEVED**
Give verbal information only once. **CONFUSION**	This involves the bus driver being told all the turns etc on the whole journey only once. **CONFUSION**	**Repeat Rephrase Recheck** This allows the information given to the bus driver is checked and clarified. **UNDERSTANDING ACHIEVED**

Talking over a busy class buzz. **CONFUSION**	This causes the bus driver only to get part of the instructions. **CONFUSION**	Make sure you have the targeted **audience's attention**. **UNDERSTANDING ACHIEVED**
Presenting too much verbal information.	The bus driver cannot remember all the verbal information regarding his destination. This can result in detours or the driver getting lost. **CONFUSION**	Provide visual clues to verbal instruction. These Act like a satnav providing additional help with the direction the bus is going. **UNDERSTANDING ACHIEVED**
Using vocabulary which is not known by the pupils. **CONFUSION**	This is like the bus driver being given the wrong ticket and he drops the passenger off at the wrong destination. **CONFUSION**	Ensure any language you are using is known by your pupils. **UNDERSTANDING ACHIEVED**
Stepping in too quickly with more verbal information as you think the pupils have not understood the first set of instructions. Information overload. **CONFUSION**	The bus gets overcrowded and the driver must offload some. This may result in keywords being lost amongst the many words. **CONFUSION**	Try **O.W.L** This allows the bus driver to hold onto the key passengers and not stop to collect more. **UNDERSTANDING ACHIEVED**

Chapter 8
Teacher Interaction Styles

Since students spend a tremendous amount of time with their teachers in the school, the relationship with a teacher can be fundamentally essential to how well understudies learn. Stable teacher-student connections were related in both the short and long haul with enhancements for higher student academic engagement, attendance, grades, low conflict behaviours, suspensions, a high degree of closeness and support, and little reliance and lower school dropout rates.

Three important skills to be developed in young children.

1. **Eye contact** (unless the child has an additional need preventing this). Look at the speaker to ensure appropriate attention is being shown.
2. **Turn-taking** – Effective communication and discussion skills require the children to learn how to take turns in a conversation. They need to know when to speak and when to listen.
3. **Active Listening** – It is important that children actively listen to the teacher and just not hear!

The following is a summary of the main adult interaction styles.

Interaction Style	Characteristics	Implications
Director Role	• Maintains tight control of the classroom and the pupils' activities. • Makes all the suggestions, gives directions and asks all the questions.	Few opportunities for the pupils to develop turn-taking skills.
Entertainer Role	Playful and lots of fun The teacher does most of the talking and playing.	Pupils have few opportunities to take an active role in their learning or communication skills.
Timekeeper Role	• Rushes through activities and lessons to stay on schedule. • Planner-driven not child-driven.	• Pupils have limited interactions. • Limited chances for active communication skills.
Too Quiet Role	• Barely interacts with pupils even when they initiate. • Sits at their desk when teaching or pupils are carrying out a task.	• No turn-taking. • No opportunities for turn-taking.
Rescuer Role	• Assumes that the child will not be able to answer. • Bombards with interruptions and offers rescuing before the child has shown any need for it.	The pupil does not have to listen to be active in their learning as a teacher will always help and continuously support.
Responsive Role	• The teacher is tuned into their pupils' needs and interests.	Lots of Eye contact • Turn-taking

	• Responds in ways that encourage the pupils to take an active part in their interactions, both with other pupils and the teacher.	• Active Listening • Active learning

Early teacher-student connections' quality has a long-lasting effect explicitly on students who had more clashes with their teachers or showed more dependency on their kindergarten teachers also had lower academic achievement and behavioural problems. Students appeared more self-directed, kind, collaborative, and more engaged in learning.

As a teacher, your aim is to become a Responsive Educator. As the name suggests learning should be a two-way process. It also suggests that effective communication is required.

Teachers do not lead learning they facilitate learning alongside the pupil.

Chapter 9
Teacher Communication Skills with Parents

Parent and teacher communication is hugely important as a child's time is predominantly between school and home life, and as a teacher – you are essentially 'the parent' away from home and children rely on you to be their moral guidance and their motivator when they are in your classroom. You oversee their education – undoubtedly one of the most important tasks in the world.

Teacher and parent communication is not just about keeping open channels for feedback, it is also the platform for starting a healthy, respectful relationship with parents that will ultimately benefit your students hugely. Once you realise that both teachers and parents want what is best for your children – then you can really begin to work together to implement it.

Factors which contribute to Effective Communication.

1. Interaction Styles
2. Listening not hearing
3. Having a good Communication Toolbox

Like the adult interaction styles, these are also applicable to communication with parents.

Director

1. Maintains tight control over the conversation.
2. Makes suggestions, gives directions and asks questions.

Impact

Parents have few opportunities to contribute to the conversation on an equal footing.

Entertainer

1. Appears very jovial.
2. Uses too much humour.

Impact

Parents may feel that the meeting is not treating the issues seriously.

Any meaningful engagement between teachers and parents is lost.

Timekeeper

1. Rushes through the conversation.
2. Focuses on the clock to stay within schedule.

Obviously timing is important in parent-teacher meeting as they usually are allocated 15-minute appointment time. Simply end the meeting by suggesting another appointment solely to discuss the remaining issue.

Impact

Limited opportunity to discuss all issues raised or required to be discussed.

Too Quiet

1. Barely interacts with the parents even when they initiate.

Impact

Parents may not feel that their concerns are being listened to or taken on board.

Rescuer

1. Assumes that the parents will not be able to express themselves.
2. Constantly interrupts providing answers and suggestions.

Impact

Parents may feel they are being controlled by the teacher or just basically give up and disconnect from the meeting.

Responsive

1. Teacher is tuned into the parents' responses and issues.

2. Responds in ways (Toolbox) that encourage active turn-taking and a meaningful discussion.

Impact

Lots of active listening and discussion takes place.

Communication Toolbox

1. Follow the other person's lead (verbal/nonverbal).
2. Be aware and show interest in what the other person is saying/doing.
3. Use O.W.L
4. Nod head.
5. Maintain eye contact!
6. Paraphrase some of the other person's comments
7. Summarise the main points of discussion.
8. Summarise the final agreement and any actions to be undertaken.
9. Use vocabulary which can be understood by parents i.e., no educational mumbo jumbo!
10. Invite parents to put their thoughts first then apply as a teacher.

Four Vital Statements for meeting parents

1. Observe – Be aware of the tone and non-verbal behaviour of parents. This will help gauge how the parents are feeling.
2. Focus – Do not do anything else while listening. Full attention should be given to the speaker.

3. Acknowledge – Acknowledge the parents' point of view, even if you do not agree with it. Once this has been done then an opposing explanation can be stated.
4. Respect

Let the parents begin the conversation and NEVER interrupt.

Some wise words:

"Communication works for those who work at it."

"We have two ears and one mouth so that we can listen twice as much as we speak."

Chapter 10
Effective Teaching and Learning Top 10 Tips

1. Celebrate Children's Success.
2. Effective Planning Consistency.
3. Robust IEP Targets/Assessment.
4. Clear differentiation reflects pupils' needs.
5. Multisensory teaching and learning.
6. Effective use of ICT in promoting independence and socialisation.
7. Effective classroom team management.
8. Pupils involved in their own learning.
9. Effective teacher evaluations.
10. Positive agreed school ethos.

In more detail:

1. Celebrate Children's Success
- Classroom and corridor displays.
- Up to date displays.
- Bright and colourful displays.
- All children displayed across the displays.
- Incentives and reward schemes.
- School Assemblies.
- Teacher/Principal Certificates.

2. Effective Planning

- Clear consistency across the school on main points of lesson planning.
- Diversity in lesson planning to meet the learning needs of all pupils.
- Planning always in place so anyone (sub teacher) can lift and deliver.
- Effective evaluation of planning.

3. Robust IEP Targets/Assessment and Testing

Clear effective assessment in place

- Developmental target setting.
- IEPs are SMART.
- Clear Review and Evaluation.
- Value Added clearly identified.
- Behaviour targets valued.
- Recognition of new EMERGENT PROFILES.
- A wide diverse range of assessment/testing.
-

4. Differentiation

- No death by worksheet for SEN pupils.
- SEN pupils should not all be doing the same work.
- Clear differentiation is obvious in planning.
- Use multisensory learning.
- Hands-on learning across all areas.

5. Multisensory Teaching

Use:

- Hands-on learning.
- Concrete activities.
- Contextualised Learning.
- ICT supported Learning.
- NOT WORKSHEETS ALL THE TIME.

6. Effective use of ICT

- Daily use of ICT.
- Flip charts.
- Online websites.
- Interactive White Board used as a teaching tool not big screen.
- Use cameras and other ICT.
- Pupils very aware of e safety
-

7. Effective Classroom Teams

- Clear shared planning amongst team.
- Effective use of classroom assistants (not just photocopying!).
- Shared behaviour approaches used consistently.
- Covering teachers are aware of classes they are covering i.e., needs and specific issues.

8. Pupils active in their learning (when appropriate)

- Pupils are aware of their learning targets.
- Targets are discussed with pupils and reviewed with pupils.
- Encourage group work in class.

9. Effective Evaluation/Assessment

- Teachers should be specific in their evaluations and not general comments.
- Evaluations should feature teaching and learning.

i.e.

The topic went well, most sounds learnt. Pupils enjoyed all the activities.

SHOULD BE

Topic assisted all targets to be reached however confusion remains with sounds between v and f.

10. Strong Shared School Ethos

- Shared school vision
- Shared school values
- All team members are valued.
- Mutual respect for all staff and management
- Welcoming and friendly atmosphere
- Atmosphere where pupils are celebrated.

Chapter 11
Assessment

Assessment plays an important role in any child's learning journey if it is used in a constructive way. For myself, I always felt diagnostic testing was vital to ensure the child was always at the centre.

Why test?

1. To ensure an accurate baseline is identified.
2. To ensure accurate target setting for the pupil
3. To allow value-added to be determined.
4. To clearly demonstrate progress
5. To allow success to be celebrated

Types of Assessment

1. Screening Tests (i.e., Salford Reading/Spar Spelling)
2. Diagnostic Tests (WRAPS/Staffordshire Maths)
3. Standardised Tests (PTE/PTM)
4. Classroom Based Tests
5. Psychological Tests (WISC)
6. Specialist Therapy Tests (Medical Reports/SLT Reports)

Assessment Process

1. Refer to any specialist report (Psychologist/SLT)
2. Screening Test to confirm ability age (if not recently identified)
3. Diagnostic Test (suitable to ability age)
4. Match finding to developmental learning programmes.
5. Identify the right target.

Basic Concepts of Assessment

1. To compare with the pupils' peer group, use Chronological age.
2. To obtain diagnostic information use ability age.
3. For longitudinal information use Chronological age.

Benefits of Assessment.

1. Provides clear baseline of pupil's strengths and areas for development.
2. It provides information for a psychologist when deciding further support or placement.
3. It ensures accurate and individualised target setting.
4. It enables progress to be reported and success celebrated.

Case Studies

1. Pupil X

Chronological age 13 years 8 months

Psychological Reports		Diagnostic Testing		Analysis
Reading age 7 yrs. 3 mos		WRAPS score 36 Word Recognition Age 7.0 Literacy Profile shows		Listening skills weak
Has difficulties with the following:				Reinforce sound families at en/in
phonics Sight vocabulary Ability to spell simple words		Strong on consonants		Introduce simple blends sh sl sm
		Weak vowels and substitutions		
		Staffordshire Maths raw score 46		Review 3D shapes
Maths age 7 yrs. 11 mos Has difficulties with the following:		Maths age 8.7 Subtraction horizontal within 20		Subtraction within 20 (horizontal)
Number operations Number quantity Basic number bonds Measures		Basic sets 3D shape Basic fractions		Fractions ½ and ¼ Grouping and sets

2. Pupil Y

Chronological Age 6 yrs. 8 mos

Psychological Reports		Diagnostic Tests		Analysis
Reading age <5 yrs. Development of Language Skills Listening and Attention Preforming with a group Basic Reading skills		Early Literacy Test (ELT) Total score 18 Literacy Age 4.6 Quotient <72 Percentile 3 (below)		Needs to work initially on listening skills. Phonological awareness first Simple sounds First 20 keywords
Maths age <5 Basic Number Skills Number Recognition		Basic Number Test Number age <5 yrs. Oral counting to 20 Number names to 10 Basic number order 1 – 20 Number quantity 10		Number names 1 – 10 Oral counting to 20 Making groups to 10

Assessment is today's means of modifying tomorrow's instruction!(Carol Ann Tomlinson)

Chapter 12
Engagement Not Teaching

The future of Additional Needs Educational

I was lucky during my final year as Principal to attend a training course conducted by Professor Barry Carpenter CBE.

The following are the key points I took from his remarkably interesting and thought-provoking training.

1.   Complexity of Needs

The new SEN pupil now displays more than one need and more likely several co-existing needs.

They will display a SPIKED learning profile.

The curriculum now needs to shift away from Literacy/Numeracy to Resilience and Well Being.

2.   Who are these new children?

Those who display:

- Childhood mental health issues.
- Fragile X
- Premature babies
- Foetal Alcoholic Syndrome
- Complex ASD disorders

3. What changes are needed?

- Move from a curriculum lead education to an enquiry-based education.
- Teachers will no longer say, "I have never had a child like this before," BECAUSE teachers will!

Research and Studies

4. Premature Babies

- Premature babies are surviving at a higher rate with increasing scientific discoveries.
- Studies indicate 63% have been born prematurely.
- If born at 28 weeks or before only the white matter has developed, and an incubator is a vastly different environment from a natural womb. Therefore, the brain will develop differently.
- From 28–31 weeks there is an increased likelihood of speech and language difficulties as the part of the brain responsible for speech develops during this time.

5. SEN of premature studies indicate at 11 years old.

- 66% diagnosis of ADHD
- 86% have had invasive operations and due to size, no pain killer can be given. This results in major TRAUMA.
- 10% displayed Autism.
- 93% by the age of 19 have a psychiatric diagnosis.

6. Romanian Orphanage Studies

The children in these orphanages had

- Lack of adult interaction.
- Auditory System incomplete development therefore sound system fails to develop completely.
- Lived in a dry and sterile environment.
- The comparison being made by this environment and that of an incubator.

7. Neurological Studies

- At week 24 the lobe for numerical operations has developed completely.
- Too much exposure to social media is causing a rewiring in the brain.
- Neurological implications are becoming more relevant and important in SEN.

Implication of Above Studies

Children who are now and will be coming to the attention of educators are:

Wired differently.

Learn differently.

Will need to be taught differently.

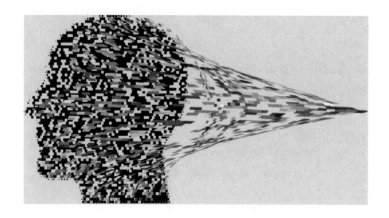

This diagram clearly shows how neurological issues and development can have a direct influence on the additional needs a child will exhibit.

8. Mental Health vs Cognitive barriers

In the future, mental health barriers will overtake cognitive barriers.

This will result in a change in the assessment profiles, teaching and the focus in special schools' curriculum.

Professor Carpenter highlighted that the SEN pupil of the twenty-first century will be:

- Not just illiterate and innumerate BUT they will be emotionally illiterate.
- Mentally vulnerable
- Have suffered either Disadvantage, Deprivation or Disability.
- Fragile learners

- Require a new approach and thinking of SEN teaching.

SEND Legislation in England and Wales promotes a new SEN Curriculum in special schools. This new curriculum consists of the following four main areas:

1. Communication and Interaction
2. Cognition and Learning
3. Mental Health
4. Sensory and Physical

I passionately believe that this is the direction that special schools should move towards to provide effective and efficient education. A major part of this new research and curriculum focuses on the increased need for an ENGAGEMENT CURRICULUM.

When a child is excluded from stimulation by either disadvantage, deprivation, or disability they become disengaged in the learning journey. This means that educators in the future need to RE-ENGAGE these pupils again.

Pupils birth history and brain scans will become part of a child's diagnostic information provided to schools in the future.

The profile of a child is complex and to meet the needs of future SEN pupils we need to.

1. Pay attention to birth history/scans/neurological issues as part of a diagnostic profile.
2. Curriculum in special schools must change and move from cognitive barriers at their centre but to mental health barriers.
3. Teachers will need to re-engage their pupils first before helping them with their learning journey.
4. The Inspectorate need to be trained and remodel their methods of inspection in special schools as their tools are too focused on cognitive barriers.

This Chinese proverb highlights the situation facing education today.

When the winds of change blow

Some people build walls.
And others build windmills.

Chapter 13
Promoting Positive Behaviour

Behaviour is anything a person does which can be observed.

Behaviour both good and bad must be learnt.

Everyone can learn new behaviour.

Behaviour which has been rewarded is more likely to be repeated.

Behaviour is influenced by what happens before it and what happens after it.

Studies show that the types of behaviour which causes adults most stress tend to be low intensity and high-frequency ones.

Over the course of my career, I have noticed there are around six different types of classroom behavioural displays by pupils. The following table shows these six different types of behaviours and suggested ways to deal with them.

Behavioural type	Strategies
Disorganised	• Proximity praise to remind the child of the next step. • Check equipment before beginning the activity. • Ask the child what he needs for the activity. • A checklist may help to make decisions. • Verbal prompts for specific activities • Organise for one activity at a time. • Teach routines for where things are kept.
Over the top	• Confront the behaviour. • Stand close to the pupil. • Speak quietly and ask him to calm down. • Calmy state expectations of behaviour and consequences. • Give a rule reminder. • Remove the sense of audience. • Be patient.
Outright Defiance	• Stay calm. • Moderate the pitch and tone of voice so that it stays low. • Stay an appropriate distance. Too close may appear threatening. • Use I statements, not you statements. • Do not get into a win or lose situation. • Offer consequences as choices
Shy	• Place with friends • Avoid over attention. • Encourage by supporting contribution to activities. • Initially, encourage small contributions. • Allow time for pupil develop confidence. • Give praise for each small achievement

Refusal to co-operate	• Calmly restate expectations. • Give the child a limited choice. • Give time to comply. • Look/move away. • Avoid confrontation. • Clarify consequences of behaviour
Dominant	• Avoid eye contact. • Share out tasks in a group. • Give feedback when the child is being quiet

Above all the pupils must be treated with dignity in all positive behaviour strategies.

"You can't teach children to behave better by making them feel worse. When children feel better, they behave better."

- Pam Leo

www.LearningStationMusic.com

Chapter 14
Resilience in Children

Happiness = G + C + V

    G = genetics

    C = circumstances

    V = things we have voluntary control over

As human beings, we have voluntary control over the following.

Positive emotions

Engagement

Relationships

Attitudes

Let us look at each one of these in turn.

Positive Emotions

Humans have the natural tendency to always see the negative.

We need to encourage children to HAVE A GO!

Rewards need to be meaningful i.e., reward the effort not the result.

Change I cannot into I can!

Relationships

Need to develop a relationship that encourages engagement and have a go mentality.

Develop the relationship of not an all-knowing teacher but more of a facilitator.

Guide, help, challenge the learning.

Develop an atmosphere of stretching and not stressing.

Develop a learning environment where making mistakes is fine – a natural part of learning and not a failure (resilience)

Meaningful

Learning should be meaningful.

Contextualise the learning.

Encourage making a choice (this develops self-esteem and self-belief

Give time to asking children their opinion as quite often there is a fear to offer an answer because it might be the wrong answer.

Attitudes:

- It is about setting appropriate goals SMART (specific, meaningful, achievable, realistic and time bound.
- Performance goals are common but TOXIC.
- We focus too much achieving the final goal i.e., right, or wrong.
- Learning goals are more appropriate i.e. I am improving
- Do your best and NOT be the best.

Chapter 15
Summary

The whole ethos of this book is to share what ideas, theories, or activities which I found most useful in the classroom. I have tried to cut through all the theories and put them into actual practice terms.

It is my hope that teachers particularly beginning teachers will find the information shared within this book useful as they start on their teaching career.

The following are a final summary of what makes:

A good lesson

A good teacher

A good school

A Good Lesson

Start by linking with previous learning.

1. Keep the lesson aims and the content simple.
2. Always check understanding before starting.
3. Remember to differentiate.
4. Use multisensory activities and not just worksheets/
5. Always have a Plenary session to check the aims are reached.

Always move around the classroom do not teach from your desk!

A Good Teacher

1. Is an encourager – encouraging self-esteem.
2. Is a gardener growing learning.
3. Is a believer developing children's self-belief.
4. Is a motivator helping children feel valued.

A Happy Child Will Learn!

A Good School is one where:

1. All the school family embrace the school ethos.
2. All staff members are valued, and their role celebrated.
3. The school is totally child centred.
4. Welcomes parents as equal partners in their child's education.
5. Be at the centre of their community.
6. Celebrate success regularly.
7. Be a home from home for its pupils.

According to M Boxall and The Six Principles of Nurture. A good school is one in which

1. Children's learning is viewed developmentally.
2. The classroom is a safe base.

3. Language in the classroom is an important form of communication.
4. Behaviour is a form of communication.
5. The importance of nurture in development and well-being.
6. The importance of transition in children's lives.

Lessons I have learnt regarding teaching over the years before starting any curricular teaching are:

1. Know your pupils.
2. Look at the whole child. Strengths and weaknesses.
3. Develop the child's self-esteem.
4. Show a child they matter, and they can achieve.

Promoting Learning

1. Set clear Learning objectives.
2. Involve the child in their own learning.
3. Help the child realise FAIL is only the first attempt in learning.
4. Use a child's strengths to build areas for development.
5. Each child is unique and has their own journey of learning.

Useful Initialisms

For any planning within the school.

A – appraise the current baseline.

P – Prioritise areas for development.

I – initiate the programme.

E – Evaluate and review progress to date.

For solving any issue.

S – search for all views and information around the issue.

O – Observe how the facts appear and are linked.

S – Solve, suggest possible solutions to the issue.

I have thoroughly enjoyed my 32 years in education. I have felt it a privilege to teach the next generations and it was never just a job but a vocation.

Like everything in life, the more you put in the more you get out! Teaching is no different. If you are to make a difference in your pupils' lives, then you cannot treat it as a job.

If it had not been for health issues, I would not have retired early. I have taught in wonderful schools ending up as Principal of a large special school.

The two most memorable moments in my career were: firstly, when I was appointed vice-principal of the primary school I attended as a child. My father and grandfather and great grandfather had all been pupils there. I was in post when the school celebrated its 150th anniversary. An incredibly special moment for all but especially for myself.

Secondly, I was appointed as Principal of a large special school. A little pupil who was unable to walk due to his condition after a year took his first few steps and gave me a hug! This summed up everything that I believed teaching is all about THE CHILD!

Whoever is reading this book, I wish them every success in their teaching career. One thing I would suggest which was suggested to me in my first year, take a photograph of each class you teach. I did this and can look back at all the wee faces who passed through my classes. It brings a big smile to my face.

When someone asks you why you want to become a teacher, tell them that every job has its ups and downs but not every job can CHANGE A LIFE FOREVER!

References

- Adult Interaction Styles – www.doodlebugs.com
- Benjamin Bloom Taxonomy – cft.vanderbilt.edu blooms taxonomy.
- Carl Rogers Facilitation Theory – Kolb's Learning Styles and Experimental Learning Cycle.
- Carl Jung – www.cgjungpage.org
- Curian M – www.curianinstitute.com
- ELKAN – Training & Resources Catalogue www.elkan.co.uk
- Gender differences in the classroom – Educational Psychology Chapter 4 Student Diversity.
- Marjorie Boxall – Nurture Groups in Schools: Principles and Practice. (2nd Edition) 2010.
- Griffiths 2012 – Learning Styles/ELT Journal Abilities and Academic Performance.
- Kolb's Learning Styles – www.simplypsychology.org
- Sternberg & Grigorenko 1997 – Styles of Thinking.